Decoding Decisions:

The Role of Neuro-Linguistic Programming in Decision-Making

By Rex Morton

Copyright Page

© 2023 by Rex Morton

Published by Omniterra Media Inc
First Edition
Visit the author's website at www.rexmorton.com
For information regarding special discounts for bulk purchases, please contact Rex Morton Publishing Special Sales at rex@rexmorton.com.

Disclaimer

This book is intended to provide information about the fields of Neuro-Linguistic Programming (NLP) and Cognitive Behavioural Therapy (CBT) and their potential integration. While the author has made every effort to ensure that the information was correct at the time of publication, the author does not assume and hereby disclaims any liability to any party for any loss, damage, or disruption caused by errors or omissions, whether such errors or omissions result from negligence, accident, or any other cause.

The contents of this book should not be used as a substitute for professional advice, diagnosis, or treatment. The reader should always consult a qualified healthcare provider about mental health concerns or conditions. Never disregard professional psychological or medical advice or delay in seeking it because of something you have read in this book.

The views expressed in this work are solely those of the author and do not necessarily reflect the views of the publisher, and the publisher hereby disclaims any responsibility for them.

Including websites, links, or references to other resources does not mean that the author or the publisher endorses the information the organization or website may provide or its recommendations. Furthermore, the author does not guarantee the accuracy of these resources' information.

The use of any information provided in this book is solely at your own risk.

Welcome to "Decoding Decisions: The Role of Neuro-Linguistic Programming in Decision-Making." This book is a journey into the fascinating intersection of Neuro-Linguistic Programming (NLP) and decision-making processes, exploring how these two domains influence and shape each other. But before we delve into the meat of the matter, it's essential to lay some groundwork.

What is Neuro-Linguistic Programming (NLP)?

Neuro-Linguistic Programming, popularly known as NLP is a psychological strategy that entails studying the tactics employed by successful people and using them to accomplish one's own objectives. Pioneered by Richard Bandler and John Grinder in the 1970s, NLP focuses on helping individuals change and improve their behaviours and decision-making processes. While it has its fair share of critics, there's no denying that NLP has had a significant impact on fields like business, sports, education, therapy, and personal development.

The Scope of the Book and Its Objectives

The primary aim of "Decoding Decisions" is to illuminate how NLP can influence, enhance, and shape decision-making processes in personal and professional contexts. This book has been designed to appeal to a broad audience, including business professionals, coaches, educators, students, and anyone interested in personal development or psychology.

The objectives of the book are as follows:

To provide a comprehensive understanding of NLP and decision-making processes.

To demonstrate how NLP techniques can be used to improve decision-making.

To highlight the practical applications of NLP in various contexts.

To discuss the ethical considerations of using NLP.

To explore the future of NLP in decision-making in light of emerging trends and technologies.

Overview of Each Chapter

To achieve these objectives, the book is divided into several vital chapters.

Chapter 1: Understanding Neuro-Linguistic Programming (NLP) delves into the roots of NLP, its fundamental principles, and the key figures who've contributed to its development.

Chapter 2: The Science of Decision-Making provides an overview of decision-making processes, theories, models, and the role of cognitive biases.

Chapter 3: NLP and Perception explores how NLP influences our perception and interpretation of reality, contributing to our decision-making processes.

Chapter 4: The Intersection of NLP and Decision-Making is the book's heart, where we delve into how NLP techniques can improve decision-making, supported by case studies and examples.

Chapter 5: NLP in Professional Contexts and Chapter 6: NLP in Personal Life discuss the application of NLP in various domains, from business and leadership to personal relationships and self-development.

Chapter 7: NLP and Ethical Considerations addresses the ethical use of NLP, potential misuse, and guidelines for its ethical application.

Finally, Chapter 8: The Future of NLP in Decision-Making, looks forward to emerging trends in NLP and decision-making, setting the stage for future research and exploration.

I will summarize the key points from each chapter, offering final thoughts on the role of NLP in decision-making.

I hope that "Decoding Decisions" will serve as a valuable guide on your journey to understanding and applying Neuro-Linguistic Programming in your decision-making processes. Now, let's embark on this exciting exploration together!

The Origins and Evolution of NLP

Neuro-Linguistic Programming (NLP) was born out of curiosity about human excellence and the desire to replicate it. In the early 1970s, Richard Bandler, a young information scientist, Gestalt therapist, and John Grinder, a linguistics professor, sought to discover the patterns behind effective communication, therapeutic, and change work.

Their work began with the modeling of exceptional communicators and therapists such as Fritz Perls (founder of Gestalt Therapy), Virginia Satir (a renowned family therapist), and later, the hypnotherapist Milton Erickson. Bandler and Grinder sought to understand the language, behaviour, and thinking patterns that made these individuals so effective in their work.

Neuro-Linguistic Programming was coined to represent the relationship between the brain and language, and patterns or programming of thought and behaviour. Over the years, NLP has evolved and expanded, influenced by other therapists, researchers, and practitioners worldwide.

Fundamental Concepts and Principles of NLP

NLP operates on a set of guiding principles and presuppositions.

Here are some key concepts:

The Map is Not the Territory: This principle suggests that everyone has a unique perspective or 'map' of the world, which is not the actual world ('territory') but rather a subjective representation. Our perceptions, beliefs, and behaviours are driven by our 'maps,' not reality.

The Body and Mind are Parts of the Same System: This principle recognizes the interconnectedness of the mind and body. Changes in one can lead to changes in the other.

People Have Everything They Need to Make Change Happen: NLP suggests that individuals inherently possess the necessary resources to effect changes in their lives. It's about uncovering and mobilizing these resources.

The Meaning of Communication is the Response To It: In NLP, effective communication is judged by the response it elicits, not by the communicator's intent.

There is No Failure, Only Feedback: This principle reframes 'failure' as an opportunity to learn and improve.

Notable Figures in NLP and Their Contributions

While Richard Bandler and John Grinder are the co-founders of NLP, many others have significantly contributed to its development.

Fritz Perls: His Gestalt Therapy influenced NLP's focus on personal responsibility and 'remaining in the present moment.'

Virginia Satir: Her work in family systems therapy highlighted the importance of communication and congruence, influencing NLP's emphasis on recognizing and improving communication patterns.

Milton Erickson: The hypnotherapist's indirect and metaphorical communication style greatly influenced NLP's language patterns.

Robert Dilts: A key developer and author in NLP, Dilts contributed to the development of 'Systemic NLP.' He also pioneered the concept of 'Logical Levels,' an invaluable tool for understanding and facilitating personal and organizational change.

Judith DeLozier and Leslie Cameron-Bandler: These women played significant roles in developing NLP, contributing to the understanding of 'submodalities' and the 'emotional intelligence' aspect of NLP.

Understanding NLP's origins, principles, and critical figures lays a foundation for exploring its application to decision-making processes. As we delve deeper into the subsequent chapters, remember that NLP is a dynamic field, continually evolving as practitioners and researchers contribute new insights and techniques.

Overview of Decision-Making Processes

Decision-making is a vital part of our daily lives. From choosing what to wear in the morning to making important business decisions, we are constantly evaluating options and making choices. The decision-making process generally involves a sequence of steps:

Identifying the Decision: Recognizing that a decision needs to be made and defining the nature of the choice.

Gathering Information: Collecting relevant data and information about the available options.

Evaluating the Options: Weighing the pros and cons of each choice.

Making the Decision: Selecting the most suitable option based on the evaluation.

Implementing the Decision: Carrying out the decision and taking necessary actions.

Reviewing the Decision: Reflecting on the decision-making process and the outcome to learn for future decisions.

Theories and Models of Decision-Making

Various theories and models aim to explain how we make decisions. Here are a few key ones:

Rational Decision-Making Model: This model presumes that individuals make decisions that are in their best interest, using all available information. It assumes perfect rationality, which is often not the case in real-world situations.

Bounded Rationality: Herbert Simon proposed this model, suggesting that people are 'satisficers.' Due to information, cognitive, and temporal constraints, they look for a workable answer rather than an ideal one.

Prospect Theory: Developed by Daniel Kahneman and Amos Tversky, this theory suggests that rather than looking at the end result, people base their decisions on the prospective value of losses and profits. It also introduces the concept of loss aversion, where losses are felt more intensely than gains.

Intuition-Based Models: These models acknowledge that not all decisions are made through a rational, step-by-step process. Sometimes, decisions are based on intuition, particularly when time is limited, or the decision is complex.

Cognitive Biases in Decision-Making

Despite our best intentions, decision-making isn't always a rational process. Cognitive biases often influence our decisions, leading to systematic errors in thinking. Here are a few examples:

Confirmation Bias: This is the propensity to look for, read, and retain information that supports our preconceived notions while dismissing the evidence to the contrary.

Anchoring Bias: This bias develops when we make decisions based mostly on the first piece of information we come across (the "anchor").

Availability Heuristic: This cognitive shortcut leads us to overestimate the likelihood of readily available events in our memory.

Hindsight Bias: Also known as the 'knew-it-all-along effect,' this bias leads us to believe that past events were predictable or obvious, even when they were not.

Understanding the science of decision-making is the first step toward improving it. In the upcoming chapters, we'll explore how Neuro-Linguistic Programming (NLP) can help us navigate these processes and biases to make better decisions.

NLP and the Construction of Reality

One of the fundamental premises of NLP is that we construct our reality based on our perceptions. Our experiences, beliefs, values, and assumptions influence these perceptions.

For example, imagine two individuals attending the same concert. One person might have a fantastic time soaking in the music and the atmosphere, creating a positive 'reality' of the event. The other person, who may not enjoy crowded places or the specific genre of music, might perceive the same concert as an unpleasant experience. Both realities are valid and are formed based on each individual's perceptions and experiences.

This understanding is vital in NLP because it highlights the potential for change. By recognizing that our reality is subjective, we open up the possibility of altering our perceptions to change our lives positively.

Sensory-Based Experience and NLP

NLP emphasizes the importance of sensory-based experience in our understanding of the world. It identifies five primary representational systems (often referred to as VAKOG) through which we experience reality: Visual, Auditory, Kinesthetic, Olfactory, and Gustatory.

We tend to favor one or two of these systems in our perception and memory. For instance, some people might predominantly rely on visual imagery ('I see what you mean'), while others might lean more towards auditory cues ('That sounds right to me') or kinesthetic feelings ('I can't get a grip on this').

Understanding this concept allows us to communicate more effectively by matching or mirroring their preferred sensory language. It also enables us to balance and expand our own sensory perceptions for a richer experience of reality.

Perception and Interpretation through the Lens of NLP

In NLP, the process of perception is often described through the 'NLP Communication Model.' According to this model, we experience the world through our senses, but this raw sensory data is filtered through our personal experiences, beliefs, values, and cultural background. These filters lead to internal representations – our interpretation of the world – which result in feelings and behaviours.

For example, let's say you're about to give a presentation at work. You see the audience (visual), hear the chatter (auditory), and feel the butterflies in your stomach (kinesthetic). Your past experiences, beliefs about your public speaking skills, and values (e.g., achieving success, avoiding failure) will filter these sensory inputs. If you've had positive experiences and believe in your ability, you might interpret the situation as an exciting challenge. If your past experiences have been negative and you doubt your skills, you might interpret the same situation as stressful and intimidating.

By understanding this process, NLP provides tools and techniques for altering our filters, changing our internal representations, and thus influencing our feelings and behaviours. The goal is not to distort reality but to create more empowering interpretations that serve us better.

How NLP Affects Decision-Making Processes

Neuro-Linguistic Programming (NLP) has a profound impact on
the decision-making processes. One of the critical insights of
NLP is that our personal experiences, beliefs, values, and
assumptions shape our perception of reality, guiding our
decisions.

For instance, if a person believes they are not good at public
speaking, this belief will influence their decision-making process
when asked to give a presentation. They may decide to avoid
the situation, delegate the task, or face it with anxiety. If,
however, they manage to change this belief through NLP
techniques, their decision-making process will adjust
accordingly. They might choose to seize the opportunity,
prepare thoroughly, and confidently give the presentation.

NLP Techniques for Improved Decision-Making

Several NLP techniques are designed to improve decision-
making processes by providing new perspectives, overcoming
negative beliefs, and enhancing communication.

Anchoring: This technique involves associating a physical stimulus (the "anchor") with a positive emotional state. For instance, a person could associate a particular posture or gesture with a state of confidence or calm. Once this association is established, the person can trigger the desired emotional state at will by using the anchor, thus enabling better decision-making in stressful situations.

Reframing: This technique involves changing how a person perceives a situation, thus enabling different emotional responses and decisions. For example, a person might view a professional challenge as a threat, causing stress and potentially leading to poor decisions. The person can lessen stress and make more wise decisions by reframing the event as a chance for development and learning.

Swish Pattern: This technique involves visualizing a sequence of events that replaces an undesirable behaviour or response with a more desirable one. This can help people make better decisions by changing their automatic responses to certain situations.

As you can see, Neuro-Linguistic Programming plays a critical role in decision-making processes. By offering techniques for altering perceptions and behaviours, NLP can help individuals and organizations make better, more informed decisions.

Neuro-Linguistic Programming in Business and Leadership

Neuro-Linguistic Programming (NLP) plays a significant role in business and leadership. Effective leadership requires excellent communication skills, the ability to influence others, and a keen understanding of one's own and other's behaviours and motivations—all areas where NLP techniques can be applied.

For instance, NLP's concept of 'representational systems (visual, auditory, kinesthetic, olfactory, gustatory) can enhance a leader's communication effectiveness. Understanding these systems can help leaders tailor their communication to match the preferred sensory language of their team members, thus improving understanding and rapport.

Additionally, NLP techniques such as 'modeling'—the process of adopting the behaviours, language, strategies, and beliefs of highly successful individuals—can be used to develop leadership skills. For example, a budding leader might model a respected leader's communication style, decision-making processes, or problem-solving strategies in their field.

Neuro-Linguistic Programming in Sales and Negotiation

In sales and negotiation, NLP techniques can be used to build rapport, understand customer needs, and influence decisions.

Rapport-building is a fundamental skill in sales and negotiation. NLP offers techniques like 'mirroring' and 'matching,' where salespeople mimic their customers' body language, vocal qualities, or language patterns to establish a connection and foster trust.

The 'Meta-Model,' an NLP technique that involves asking specific questions to clarify vague language, can be used to understand customer needs more precisely. For example, if a customer says they want a 'reliable' car, the salesperson could use Meta-Model questions to explore what 'reliable' means to the customer: Does it mean a car that requires few repairs? A car with excellent safety ratings? Or maybe a car from a brand they trust?

Neuro-Linguistic Programming in Coaching and Personal Development

NLP is widely used in coaching and personal development because it focuses on understanding and changing behaviours, beliefs, and thought processes.

Coaches often use the 'Well-Formed Outcomes' technique to help clients set effective goals. This technique involves defining goals in positive terms, ensuring they are within the client's control, specifying when and where the client wants to achieve the goal, considering the broader impacts of attaining it, and identifying the resources needed to achieve it.

'Reframing,' another NLP technique, is commonly used to help clients overcome limiting beliefs or negative thought patterns. For example, a client who is hesitant to take on new challenges due to fear of failure might be helped to reframe 'failure' as 'learning' or 'growth opportunity,' thereby changing their perspective and enabling more positive decision-making and action-taking.

NLP offers a wealth of tools and techniques that can enhance professional effectiveness in various contexts. By improving communication, influencing skills, goal-setting, and personal development, NLP can contribute to success in business, sales, negotiation, leadership, coaching, and more.

Neuro-Linguistic Programming for Personal Decision-Making

Neuro-Linguistic Programming (NLP) offers valuable tools for enhancing personal decision-making. For instance, the NLP technique known as the 'Disney Strategy,' inspired by the creative process of Walt Disney, involves adopting three distinct perspectives - the Dreamer, the Realist, and the Critic - to generate, plan, and evaluate ideas. This technique can help individuals make more balanced, well-considered decisions by ensuring that all aspects of a decision are explored.

For example, someone considering a career change could first adopt the Dreamer perspective to envision their ideal job, then switch to the Realist perspective to plan the practical steps needed to achieve this goal, and finally take on the Critic perspective to anticipate potential obstacles and devise strategies to overcome them.

Enhancing Relationships through Neuro-Linguistic Programming

NLP can also be a powerful tool for enhancing relationships. Techniques such as 'mirroring' and 'matching' can build rapport and foster mutual understanding. In a conversation, **subtly** mirroring the other person's body language, tone of voice, or choice of words can create a sense of connection and empathy.

Furthermore, the NLP concept of 'love languages' can be used to improve romantic relationships. According to this concept, different people express and receive love differently. Some people prefer verbal expressions of love, others appreciate acts of service, and others value physical touch, quality time, or gifts. Understanding and accommodating one's own and one's partner's love languages can enhance communication, mutual understanding, and satisfaction in a relationship.

Overcoming Personal Obstacles with Neuro-Linguistic Programming

NLP offers numerous techniques for overcoming personal obstacles, such as fears, phobias, limiting beliefs, and harmful habits.

For example, the 'Fast Phobia Cure' is an NLP technique designed to reduce or eliminate phobias. This technique involves visualizing the phobic situation from a detached, third-person perspective, which can help to desensitize the individual to the feared stimulus.

Another technique, known as 'Belief Change,' can be used to overcome limiting beliefs. This technique involves identifying the belief, exploring its origin, considering its impact, and creating and reinforcing a new, empowering belief.

For instance, someone who believes "I am bad at math" might explore how this belief originated, consider how it has affected their academic or career choices, and then create a new belief such as "I can learn and improve in math with practice." Through repeated affirmation and evidence gathering (such as successful experiences in learning math), the new belief can gradually replace the old one, thereby removing the obstacle and enabling the individual to pursue new opportunities.

Neuro-Linguistic Programming offers many tools and techniques to enhance personal decision-making, relationships, and personal growth. By helping individuals understand and change their thought patterns, behaviours, and emotional responses,

NLP can empower individuals to overcome obstacles, achieve their goals, and improve their quality of life.

The Ethical Use of Neuro-Linguistic Programming in Decision-Making

Neuro-Linguistic Programming (NLP) can significantly enhance decision-making processes by providing deeper insight into our perceptions, beliefs, and behaviours. However, its power to influence perception and behaviour also carries ethical implications. The ethical use of NLP involves applying it in a way that respects individual autonomy, dignity, and well-being.

For example, an ethical application of NLP in decision-making might involve using it to help someone overcome a phobia, boost self-confidence, or improve communication skills. In each of these cases, NLP empowers the individual and enhances their quality of life, respecting their autonomy and dignity.

Potential Misuses and Abuses of Neuro-Linguistic Programming

NLP can also be misused or abused due to its influence on perception and behaviour. For instance, it could be used manipulatively in a sales or negotiation context, using NLP techniques to unduly influence a customer's or opponent's decisions.

Consider a scenario where a salesperson uses NLP techniques to create a sense of rapport and trust with a customer, then uses these techniques to convince the customer to buy a product that they don't need or can't afford. This would be an unethical use of NLP, as it manipulates the customer's decision-making process for the salesperson's benefit, violating the customer's autonomy and potentially causing harm.

Guidelines for Ethical Application of Neuro-Linguistic Programming

To ensure the ethical application of NLP, practitioners should adhere to a set of guidelines:

Respect for Autonomy: NLP should be used to empower individuals, not manipulate them. This means respecting each person's right to make their own decisions, even if they differ from the practitioner's expectations or desires.

Do No Harm: NLP techniques should be applied to promote the individual's well-being and avoid causing harm. This includes considering the potential impacts of changing a person's perceptions or behaviours and ensuring that any changes are in the person's best interest.

Informed Consent: Before applying NLP techniques, practitioners should ensure that the individual understands the nature of the methods, the purpose of their use, and the potential outcomes. The individual should then be allowed to consent to use these techniques freely.

Professional Competence: Practitioners should only apply NLP techniques in which they have been adequately trained, and they should continue to enhance their competence through ongoing education and professional development.

By adhering to these guidelines, practitioners can ensure that they are using NLP ethically, respecting individual autonomy, promoting well-being, and upholding the field's professional standards.

Thank you for reading this book. I hope you learned how NLP can help you in your decision-making process, whether for work or personal life.

I encourage you to explore my other books for insightful steps on better decision-making.

Cheers

Rex Morton

About the Author

Rex Morton is a renowned author and researcher in the United Kingdom with a passionate interest in the human mind, specifically in Cognitive Behavioural Therapy (CBT) and Neuro-Linguistic Programming (NLP).

Morton has spent a considerable portion of his professional life diving deep into the theories and principles that form the backbone of these two compelling fields.

Although Morton does not have clinical experience, his intense curiosity and dedication to studying these subjects have made him a respected figure in the field. He has thoroughly researched the integration of NLP techniques into CBT, offering fresh perspectives and insights into how these two methodologies can complement each other to enhance understanding of human cognition and behaviour.

As an author, Morton has successfully communicated his knowledge and passion to a broader audience, making complex psychological theories accessible to professionals and interested laypersons. His writing is characterized by a clear, engaging style and a focus on the practical application of theories, making them relevant to everyday life.

In his personal life, Morton is an ardent lover of the natural world, often spending his free time exploring the British countryside. His passion for landscape photography allows him to capture and share the beauty of these excursions. Despite his accomplishments, Morton is known for his humility and eagerness to continue learning. His work continues to inspire those interested in the intricate workings of the human mind and the exciting possibilities presented by the integration of NLP and CBT.

If you've found the content of this book enlightening and wish to continue your journey of understanding the human mind, I warmly invite you to visit my website at www.rexmorton.com. The website serves as a hub of knowledge where I share my latest findings, thoughts, and insights on NLP and related topics.

I also encourage you to subscribe to the newsletter available on the website. By subscribing, you'll receive regular updates on a range of topics, from detailed discussions on specific NLP techniques and their application in other fields to the latest research.

The newsletter is also the first place I'll share news of upcoming releases. Whether it's the announcement of a new book, the launch of an online course, newsletter subscribers will be the first to know. This is a great opportunity to continue learning directly from me, deepening your understanding of NLP and related topics, and enhancing your skills in applying these techniques in your own life or professional practice.
I'm looking forward to sharing this journey with you.